Silent Whispers Beneath the Moon's Glow

M VYSHNAVI SREE

INDIA • SINGAPORE • MALAYSIA

Authors Note

Yayyy!!! It's my first poem, I went running all around my house screaming and shouting. My joy knew no bounds after I wrote me very first poem.

Reading books nor writing was never my cup of tea. I never liked to sit before books for a long period of time, months together. But when I reached high school I was very fasinated to write articles because it would be given for the school magazine. Seeing my classmates getting selected for different literature activities made me grow intrest in in writing. So after my 10th maybe in the month of August I wrote my first poem "POTRAIT OF THE SOUL". Writing poetry helped me to vent out my feelings and emotions. Slowly I started to mould words into sentences and then tried rhyming with each other.

My friends and family supported and encouraged me to write. I really thank my parents M.SREE VANI AND M.VASU DEVA SHARMA for always being my cheerleaders. Not to forget my biggest thank you to all my english teachers who had thought me to improve my language skills.A very big thank you to my High school English teacher MISS RACHEL DANIEL who always helped me and supported me by correcting my mistakes.A special thanks to NOTION PRESS TEAM for making my dream book happen.

Above everything and everyone I would thank God for giving me this wonderful ability to write. At last a big thank you to all my lovely readers for giving time to read my book.

I am sure you will all connect to it.

Jai Shree Ram....

Dedicated to

This book is dedicated to every single being out there.

To every hand that picked up my book a very big thank you

To every mouth that made an effort to read my book a very big thank you.

I am sure this book will surely connect you to every emotion existing.

Contents

Contents

Contents

Poetry

Poetry is an essence of venting out your heart and soul on a piece of paper.

M.VYSHNAVI SREE

#1 "Portrait of the Soul"

I know I am not beautiful by face,

but pretty enough by heart.

I know I am not the perfect of all,

but can try out things toughest of all.

I know I do sin,

but I am not the devil.

I know I am good,

but I am not an angel.

I know I don't have those eyes, nose or maybe that look,

but all I know is GOD created me in the best way and what I am is what

DEFINES ME !!!

#2 "We Bow Down to You"

Teacher, the guiding stars we bow down to you!!

You are the light in the dark,

who make us shine in every landmark. You paint our minds with wisdom,

and our hearts with love.

Teacher, the guardian of knowledge we bow down to you!!

You teach us with a whole lot of determination,

without showing a bit of hesitation.

You explain us one, two, three and a thousand times

until we grasp and the time flies.

Teacher, the masters of classroom we bow down to you!!

Your sleepless nights correcting our mistakes,

made us perfect in every concept.

At the end of the day you make us happy,

that's the reason you are called to be

precious .

#3 "Agony of the Heart"

Cry out loud and hard

Until your heart lest goes the pain,

And your heavy tears drain.

Calm down and bear

Until your heart is ready to fight,

And you see out days clear and bright.

Gather up all your courage and boldness

To find out ways in every hardest breath,

And turn out to be the strongest wreath.

Build up hope and strength

To forget every thorn that pricked you,

And emerge out as a beautiful anew.

#4 "City of Pride"

In the hearts of Deccan figure, Hyderabad lies on the banks of Musi river.

Dotted with small hills,

To the highest being the banjara hills.

Religions unite, hand in hand,

Devotion and faith lie on every land. Temples being the symbol of cheer, where there is no place to fear.

Biryani's aroma filled in every lane, Fusion of flavors and taste of tradition beyond compare.

Tinkling of bangles to be aware,

Fragrant perfumes everywhere.

Hyderabad,city that never sleeps at night,

Where dreams always take flight.

Every lane, every corner has a story untold,

A city of pride a city of lofty heights.

#5 "Whispers of the Universe"

Knock Knock,

Who's there, Tada!!! came the SUN, always there to shine bright on you.

Knock Knock,

Who's there, Tada!!! came the MOON, always there to show you way in the dark.

Knock Knock ,

Who's there, Tada!!! came the STARS, always there to dream with you.

Knock Knock ,

Who's there, Tada!!! came the RAIN, always there to hide your tears

Knock Knock,

Who's there, Tada!!! came the UNIVERSE,

always there with open arms to hug you.

#6 "The First Drop of Rain"

It was the first drop of rain,

when the parched earth felt new again. Every plant every tree quenched their thirst,

while corners of every place were drenched.

The barren ground let out a sigh in relieve,

knowing that his amazing friend wouldn't deceive.

Every droplet gave a hope so deep,

that never made the earth sleep.

After a long lasting rain,

those beautiful gray clouds turned plain.

It was time for the daystar to shine up bright,

making the earth feel joy and delight.

With a bit of rain and sunshine,

comes the rainbow of all time.

Red, orange, yellow a total of seven, making the place feel like heaven.

#7 "The Leaping Ledegend"

Called the son of wind,who's free from death,

strength unmatched, courage untold,

Power unseen while love unshown

A hero resides whose name brings joy.

In the path of darkest night,

he will be your guiding light.

The one who leads you from wrong to right,

The one who saves you with all his might.

Defender of truth and destroyer of sin,

at times of fear he will be your friend to cheer

From Lanka's shore to Himalayan heights

his name echos loud and bright.

He is the only reason for every happiness,

and he will be the only reason for every success.

In every struggle and every pain

he will hold your hand and help you sustain.

In every prayer and every plea,

in every chant and every heart he'll always be.

Heart so pure and gentle soul,

in his name our faith never fades.

#8 "Rains"

The night grew

darker and darker,

while the moon veiled

deeper and deeper.

Beautiful sky wrapped

in the night kings' embrace,

brought the most awaited rains.

Winds of solitude howled

through the stormy night,

as thunder and lightning

echoed through the sight.

Droplets of water

scattered in a clear view,

that time of the year

when the earth felt new.

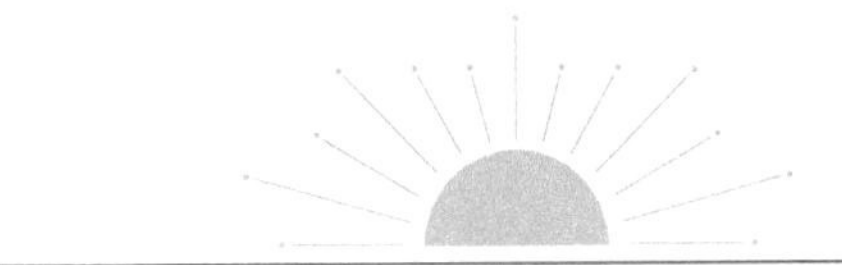

#9

If people around are not liking you then that isn't
your fault

but if you start disliking

yourself because of those

so called people,

then the fault lies in you.

#10 "A Path to An Endless Journey"

On a harsh evening of winter,

moonlight glowed softly,

and a gentle breeze howled wildly, bringing an intense feeling of solitude.

He walked through the empty streets, looking at the beautiful night sky

while tears fell apart in silence,

he whispered, his heart filled pain.

She walked through the rose filled garden,

looking at a beautiful rose

while tears fell apart in silence,

she struggled to tell her pain.

Two people bound with one soul,

 carried pain in every step,

as they walked alone in SHADOWS OF suffering,

dreaming of a path to an endless journey they dreamt.

#11 "The Call of Nature"

Deep down in forest's embrace,

when god showed man some grace.

Small tiny little green seeds,

grew out to be trees for everyone's needs.

After seasons of sun and rain,

comes new life fresh and green again. With a huge body strong enough to handle all pain,

trees stand out tall with all their might with no complain.

Long, brown slender like branches display,

hundreds of leaves that sway.

A wide range of flowers bloom bright,

 all time every day and every night.

#12 "In Your Absence"

A day did I not think of you!

Every morning every night,

every rain and every thunder

Longing your name

under the tree I wonder.

A day did I not think of you!

War of silence in my mind,

battles of emotions in my heart.

Every storm that hit me reminded you,

echoes of laughter and tears of joy were true.

A day did I not think of you!

Millions of miles apart,

but always close to heart.

Until we reunite under the light,

I'll hold all those memories tight.

#13 "Her"

they asked how did she look...

the glow in her eyes

painted the oceans blue,

pink on her cheeks made

those flowers blush anew.

her fragrance danced softly

through the air,

while the night sky

stole her bliss, unaware.

Her beauty made the moon shy,

for he slipped beneath the clouds,

and her presence made the stars

dim their spark.

      The daughter replied.......

#14 "Mahadev"

One fine day, you wake to see,

You're no longer alive, yet you are free.

Your soul has left,your body still,

Mind in a confusion, not sure of what's real.

Only thing you see is chaos all around,

People weeping until their hearts cold

You can't calm them, for your breath has ceased,

No voice no feeling can be released.

They take you to the grave, your final place,

as the sun begins to leave it's trance.

People return and pray

Leaving you alone with fear and dismay.

Then comes a hand strong and kind ,

to calm your confused mind.

The only hand that wipes your tears,

the only presence, that keeps you away from fears.

You are left lone with all pain.

but he remains just to explain,

that your not alone in the dark night,

for he is there to hold you tight.

He's called the one who lives in the grave,

and the one who rides the bull.

But did you ever realise,after all you've known

He is the only one who never leaves you alone.

He carries both fire and snow at once,

the one who tames the lion and cow without any fuss.

Not called simply a GOD or a dev

But always known as devon ka dev "MAHADEV".

#15 "The Night King"

On a cold day after a rainy night,

I lay under the moonlight

asking him how it feels like

to be alone without any guide.

With a huge face of smile and pride

he answered with all his might,

being alone made him shine bright.

The night became more beautiful

because of his presence

and showed no value

on the day of his absence.

Although with a mark on his face,

he seemed to be awesome

and made the group of stars twinkle

in cosmic blossom.

#16

In ENGLISH we say I LOVE YOU

But in poetry……..

I wish I were the moon,

so that every night

I could hear you gently whisper

to me …..

#17 "Love that's Hidden"

Isn't this called love?

How beautiful it is when the sun so bright, die's,

to let his moon shine every night.

Despite the fact of being mighty and strong,

always had his love along.

Isn't this called love?

How beautiful it is when brown roots dark and unseen,

make the plants stand upright and green.

Those that lie underground,

work in perfect silence with no sound.

Isn't this called love?

How beautiful it is when those heavy clouds with pain,

drench the parched earth wet with rain.

Although with a whole lot of tears,

never did they complain about their fears.

Isn't this called love?

How beautiful it is when the whispers of the wind mear,

fill the planet's atmosphere with music that's clear

With love and joy as the world seems to sway,

every little thing tells an awesome story of yesterday

#18 "One Life"

Live your life, chase your dreams,

set your goals

let the world hear your screams

Coz there's no one who'll do it for you.

In every rain, In every storm

Through every night and every light

shine bright like a burning star

with all your might coz that's just you..

In every step, you may fall,

don't be afraid,

Wake up, fold your sleeves

Grab a drink and run down to chase your dreams.

Every smile, every breath

and every beat

is a brand new start

For every moment is a second chance

So do it now, for no regrets

Coz there's just one life......

#19 "Never did I Know"

Never did I know I would be a poet until
Feelings of my heavy heart,
turned out to be beautiful words of art.
Those emotions that spilled like rain,
drenched every page of mine with pain.

Never did I know I would be a poet until
I knew silence had more impact,
than actual words that could attract.
Those thoughts ruining my mind,
became roots of my actions' bind.

Never did I know I would be a poet until

I could taste the bitterness of my tears,

and strengthened myself at the time of fears.

While those beautiful stars of the night,

showed me way through their light.

Never did I know I would be a poet until

Every stone and every rock I touched,

had a beautiful story that blushed.

Every leaf and every petal I saw, sway,

told awesome stories of yesterday.

#20 "Logic Over Emotion"

On a cold thunderstorm night,

weeping under the moon light,

while tears drop apart,

I wonder why is it always

mind over heart

Minds filled with logic,

while heart with emotion,

tides of same ocean,

yet so tragic.

Minds not man's fool,

heart blinded with love

that's meant to rule

in the storm where emotions sway logic guides our way.

#21

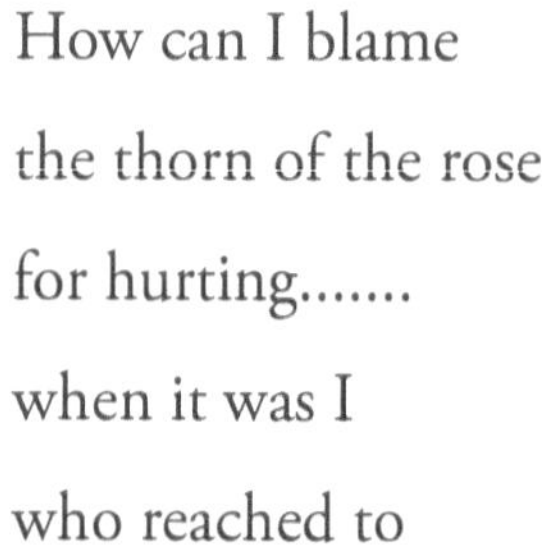

How can I blame

the thorn of the rose

for hurting.......

when it was I

who reached to

PLUCK it.......

#22 "Ink-Stained Journeys"

Running up through the stairs

never seemed to ache,

but getting down on the last day

was hard enough to take.

Classrooms filled with love and gossips,

corridors echoed with laughter and noise,

fear of maths and love for english was a blast,

but never did we think time to leave

was way too fast.

Classrooms never mentioned by grade,

for each held a lovely name,

some being called the naughtiest

while some called the neighbours of staff room,

never felt offended but always proud.

It seemed to be a twelve year roller coaster

that ended within a blink,

Beautiful tear stained eyes left crying,

the first looked lovely but the last

carried memories to cherish for lifetime.

#23 "F.R.I.E.N.D."

In the journey of life and existence

covered with hurdles and challenges

there's a light of presence and guidance

always by your side to enhance.

A race that's too long and weary

days filled with boredom and doubt

but does all that really matter?

when you have a dear friend always about.

On the day of success when you are

surrounded with wishes and love

all way turning back you see the day

of failure and pain, he was the only one who turned

out to stay.

When life's a whole lot of mess

and on the road of struggle and fear

A friend indeed a buster of stress

is always by your side to cheer.

#24 "Light of His Reign"

For a bird who cannot talk,

is protected while sleeping in the nest

so are you not,as you walk,

in the shadows of fear and quest.

For a blind who cannot see,

Is protected in all seasons

So are you not, as you dream

to be the best for all reasons.

For a man who lives in the dark,

Is protected from all even and pain

so are you not, as you bark

In the light of his reign.

#25 "Unspoken Desires"

In an ocean of blue eyes,

you are the best view captured.

In a galaxy of stars,

you are the moon adored.

In garden of the heart,

you are a red rose blooming.

In a forest of thoughts occupied,

you are the every battle fought for.

In the desert of hot sun,

you are a shade for shadows made.

In the melody of soul,

you are an emotion of love and joy.

In the world of darkest night,

you are a hope of charming light.

In this chapter of life,

you are a guide always by my side.

#26 "A Moment of Pride"

On a friday morning of sunny bliss,

while golden beams radiate from the sun,

the huge star peeped through the clouds,

did you notice?

 Oh! what a day, a day full of fun.

The clock struck nine,

while on the ground gathered our annites,

Yellow, purple, red and green were the colours

oh,so fine! hand in the hand

the whole school unites.

The guest of honor graced us,

along with the parents of the cabinet, near,

Their faces carried a joyful fuss,

Oh! what a day, a day filled with cheer.

It all started in the name of the LORD,

as the school marched in perfect coordination,

Young leaders led the group forward,

Oh! What a day, it was a mind-blowing sensatio...

#27 "One Fine Day"

To those deep blue eyes

that bear a mountain of pain,

and for a lovely heart

that bleeds with sorrow's strain,

one fine day, those heavy clouds

of grief will burst

and so will happiness flow,

to quench your thirst.

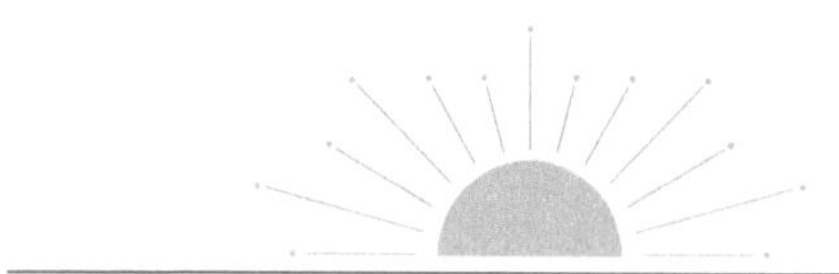

#28 "When White Aprons Turned Red"

A girl of teen chubby and brown,

down through the village

Came to the town,

with a whole lot of desire and courage.

She was a girl strong enough and bold

Oh? Pardon, did I not mention her intelligence,

it was not less than what people around told

as she hit every downfall with her excellence.

In the world of hundred choices,

she dreamt of being a saving hand

all she wished for is to raise her voice

for the poor and needy, she loved taking a stand.

She knew her road to success was way too long

but never did she give up on her dream,

for she had her family and friends along

with desire and hope as a team.

A day normal for you and me,

but tragedy that hit her was unbelievable

for she pleaded them to set her free,

none cared to listen to her cries that were incredible.

That time of her life when she lost hope,

as all her dreams shattered in no time,

in silence, she struggled to cope,

praying for solace in rhythm and rhyme.

On that silent night of silver stars abate,

cruel monsters dragged her dead.

Little did she know her fate

while white aprons turned RED.

#29 "Into An Endless Sleep"

One fine day, you wake to see

your body still, but spirit free.

The sense of touch now slips away,

for life has left, and you can no longer stay.

In the grave your place is set,

As shadows fall, the sun has set.

With broken heart and heavy eyes they weep

As you drift into an endless sleep.

Now your soul has risen, light as air,

No more pain and sorrow to bear.

None, but one stays up all night,

With tear filled eyes until dawn's next light.

#30 "A Promise for Lifetime"

In the darkest of night,

I'll be your moon shining bright.

For a war between life and death

I'll be an armor to save your breath.

Flying high in the sky above the clouds,

above the eagles and so the ravens

Together, we will touch

those lovely gates of heaven.

In my heart, you will be,

always and forever ruling my throne,

and I'll be there to serve your honor.

Your presence lights up my world

for in your eyes, you hold the spark

You will always be my dawn and dusk

as you lie in every single breath of mine.

Hold my hand darling, and never will I part,

for you shall be my girl and I'll be your man.

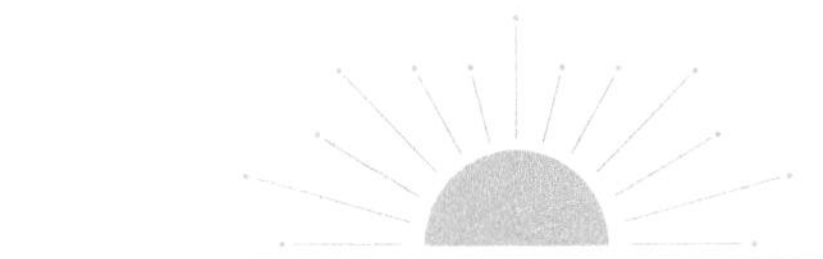

#31

In ENGLISH we say

YOU ARE MINE

But in poetry ......

You are the spark which my eyes hold,

and the smile my face wears.

#32 "Voice of the Heart"

Have you ever wondered,

is heartbreak really

heart breaking?

For we learnt heart is a soft tissue,

but did you ever think,

How can it break?

Yes, you're right.

It breaks because it is soft.

At times when you are surrounded

by people, but still you feel alone,

at times when you want to share your

thoughts but have none,

at times when your loved ones betray.

That's when the heart breaks,

Isn't it the hardest of things to handle,

deep down, it shatters with no sound

in silence carrying all the pain.

#33 "Shadows of Suffering"

People point out on the number of fears,
but nobody sees those countless tears.
They always wish to see what they require,
and collect the ones they think inspire.

They never try to mind their own business,
which tends to cause immense of illness.
They laugh out on your wrongs,
and point out on your flaws.

Those hundreds of efforts you put in are not cared,

the amount of time spent is not spared.

At the end they only see what they want,

and leave us when we want.

#34 "The Hand above You"

Nobody knows this part, the painful part.

They don't see you struggle,

nor the hard work you put in.

They judge you for being you

and blame you for being someone else.

You know the hard work you are putting in,

but you know that's very less.

You know you are not dying,

but it's not less than that either.

You still push yourself to do better

Gather your courage,

build up hope,

and still you FAIL.

The last thing you do is kneel before him,

surrender yourself,

and then you find yourself

the most ATTRACTIVE of all.

Never fear on your lows.

There's always a mighty

Hand above you

to lift you up.

#35 "A Trap"

Isn't it a trap,
To over-love or to over-care
for someone who doesn't even
acknowledge your existence?
Everyday and every night craving
for their presence,
as every dawn and every dusk
whispers a hope so deep.
In the silence of night,
when silver stars twinkle
in cosmic blossom,

I sit back wishing my old self

for how peaceful was I.

Now I've become a river

forever chasing the sea,

yet their absence has become

a part of me.

#36

In ENGLISH we say I MISS YOU

But……

In poetry we say

My eyes lost their shine,

while my heart forgot it's beat

from the time you left……..

#37 "The Best View"

What else could be more beautiful than this...

A dead dark sky, painted deep black,

With only the sound of your breath, in and out,

By the riverside, hundreds of people wait, Patient and calm, hearts filled with love.

Each gaze holds a quiet hope, so deep,

and, after a long, gentle wait,

You see the Ganga Aarti begins.

In that moment, every pain fades, Every sorrow melts into light.

For here is a view beyond words,

For here is a view captured in your eyes forever.

A beauty that lives in the soul.

 If I ever write about love, Its just Banaras, my beloved.

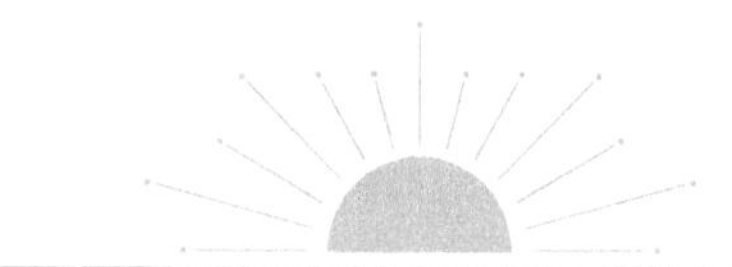

#38 "An Annite Forever"

When I was four year old,
Holding my mom's hand,
I entered those lovely gates with fear.
With a bag that was more than my height,
Crying and weeping, clinging tight.

Tears rolled down through my eyes
New faces, strange places and too many cries.
In a crowd of people unknown
I tried searching for a face known.

Tiny chairs and tiny toys too bright

Yet nothing seemed to be right

But within no time, fears began to fade,

As new friendships were soon made.

Years passed by with love and joy

Those were the days we could fully enjoy

Days when wearing a captain badge was a pride

Guiding our group with hearts open and wide.

Through the campus we ran with dreams aside

Holding hands side by side

Friendships deepened, although some would part

But every goodbye strengthened my heart.

Then arrived middle school,

With a whole lot of rules

In a path of struggle, I stumbled and grew

Faced challenges but soon learned to get through.

High school was no more fun

As COVID struck and I was done

It was not at all the same anymore,

Everything was learned behind a closed door.

However it was all together a fourteen year rollercoaster

That ended just within a blink of an eye

Holding my mom's hand, I entered with fear

But now this became a place that's forever dear.

Thank You

M.VYSHNAVI SREE